RYE FREE READING ROOM

FLOOD RELIEF 2007

Purchased with
Generous Community Support
After the Flood of 2007

**Thank You!**

# Rookie
## Read-About® Holidays

# Columbus Day

## By Christina Mia Gardeski

**Consultants**

Nanci R. Vargus, Ed.D.
Primary Multiage Teacher
Decatur Township Schools, Indianapolis, Indiana

Katharine A. Kane, Reading Specialist
Former Language Arts Coordinator,
San Diego County Office of Education

Children's Press®
A Division of Scholastic Inc.
New York  Toronto  London  Auckland  Sydney
Mexico City  New Delhi  Hong Kong
Danbury, Connecticut

Designer: Herman Adler Design
Photo Researcher: Caroline Anderson
The photo on the cover of this book shows a float of the *Santa Maria* in the Columbus Day Parade in New York City.

**Library of Congress Cataloging-in-Publication Data**

Gardeski, Christina Mia.
    Columbus Day / by Christina Mia Gardeski.
      p. cm. — (Rookie read-about holidays)
    Includes index.
    Summary: Explore the history, meaning, and customs of Columbus Day in this introductory book.
    ISBN 0-516-22371-2 (lib. bdg.)    0-516-26310-2 (pbk.)
    1. Columbus Day—Juvenile literature. 2. Columbus, Christopher— Juvenile literature. 3. America—Discovery and exploration—Spanish— Juvenile literature. I. Title. II. Series.
  E120 .G25   2001
  394.264—dc21

                                  00-046591

10 R 10 09 08 07        62

# Are you an explorer?

Explorers travel to new places.

# They meet new people and find new things.

Christopher Columbus was an explorer. We celebrate a holiday named after him.

# October 2007

| Sunday | Monday | Tuesday | Wednesday | Thursday | Friday | Saturday |
|--------|--------|---------|-----------|----------|--------|----------|
|        | 1      | 2       | 3         | 4        | 5      | 6        |
| 7      | 8      | 9       | 10        | 11       | 12     | 13       |
| 14     | 15     | 16      | 17        | 18       | 19     | 20       |
| 21     | 22     | 23      | 24        | 25       | 26     | 27       |
| 28     | 29     | 30      | 31        |          |        |          |

Columbus Day comes every year on the second Monday in October.

8

Columbus lived more than five hundred years ago in Europe (YOOR-up). He had a job there making maps.

But Columbus liked sailing better than mapmaking.

Columbus dreamed of sailing to a land called Asia (AY-shuh).

He thought he would find gold and spices there.

Gold

Spices

Long ago, it was hard to get to Asia from Europe. Explorers sailed east. Then they crossed deserts and mountains.

Columbus thought it would be easier to sail west. He would make a circle all the way around the world.

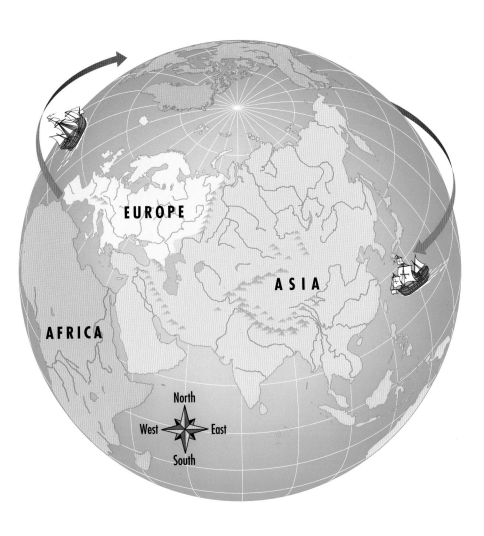

EUROPE

ASIA

AFRICA

North
West ✦ East
South

King Ferdinand

Queen Isabella

14

Columbus asked King Ferdinand and Queen Isabella of Spain to help him sail to Asia.

The king and queen gave Columbus three ships.

Columbus's ships were called the *Niña* (NEEN-ya), the *Pinta*, and the *Santa Maria* (SAN-tuh ma-REE-uh).

Columbus and his crew sailed far out into the ocean. Many days passed before they saw land.

Finally, on October 12,
1492, Columbus landed
on an island (EYE-land).

He thought he was in India, a country in Asia. Columbus called the people he met "Indians."

Columbus did not know that he was not in Asia! He was in the Bahamas.

The Bahamas are a group of islands just off the coast of the United States.

21

The people Columbus called "Indians" were really Native Americans.

They lived in America long before Columbus arrived.

The Bahamas are in the
ocean between North
America and South America.
That's why some people say
that Columbus discovered,
or found, America.

Columbus was not the first
person to discover America.
But he did find a new way
to sail to other lands.

On Columbus Day,
many towns and cities
have parades.

People wear uniforms
and colorful costumes.
Bands play music.

Columbus Day reminds us that exploring is important.

You never know what you might find!

# Words You Know

Bahamas

Christopher Columbus

King Ferdinand

Queen Isabella

Native Americans

parade

ships

31

# Index

# About the Author

Christina Mia Gardeski is a writer and editor of children's books. She is forever grateful to her parents for encouraging her love of reading and writing.

# Photo Credits

Photographs ©: AP/Wide World Photos/Marty Lederhandler: cover; Corbis-Bettmann: 27 (Kevin Fleming), 21, 30 top left (Philip Gould), 5 (Robert Maass), 14 right, 18, 30 bottom right; North Wind Picture Archives: 8, 14 left, 17, 19, 22, 30 bottom left, 31 bottom, 31 top left; PhotoEdit/Robert Brenner: 26, 31 top right; Stock Boston: 29 (Ira Kirschenbaum), 3 (Margaret Ross); Superstock, Inc.: 6, 30 top right (A.K.G. Berlin), 11; Viesti Collection, Inc./Dan Peha: 4.

Illustrations by Bob Italiano.